CONTRARIWISE

POETRY BOOKS BY SUSAN TERRIS

Contrariwise (2008)
Marriage License (2007)
Sonya, the Doll-Wife (2007)
Block Party (2007)
Natural Defenses (2004)
Poetic License (2004)
Fire Is Favorable to the Dreamer (2003)
Susan Terris: Greatest Hits (2000)
Minnesota Fishing Report (2000)
Eye of the Holocaust (1999)
Angels of Bataan (1999)
Curved Space (1998)
Killing in the Comfort Zone (1995)

CONTRARIWISE

SUSAN TERRIS

TIME BEING BOOK**S**
POETRY IN SIGHT AND SOUND

An imprint of Time Being Press
St. Louis, Missouri

Time Being Books® is an imprint of Time Being Press®, St. Louis, Missouri.

Time Being Press® is a 501(c)(3) not-for-profit corporation.

Time Being Books® volumes are printed on acid-free paper.

ISBN 978-1-56809-115-0 (paperback)

Library of Congress Cataloging-in-Publication Data:

Terris, Susan.
    Contrariwise / by Susan Terris — 1st ed.
      p. cm.
    ISBN: 978-1-56809-115-0 (pbk. : alk. paper)
        1. Carroll, Lewis, 1832–1898—Characters—Poetry. I. Title.
    PS3570.E6937C66 2008
    811'.54—dc22

                                                    2007043527

Cover design by Jeremy Thornton
Cover artwork, "La Bourrique," by William Bouguereau, appears courtesy of the
    Berkshire Museum, Pittsfield, Massachusetts
Author photograph by Susan Terris
Book design and typesetting by Trilogy Mattson and Sheri Vandermolen

Manufactured in the United States of America

First Edition, first printing (2008)

ACKNOWLEDGMENTS

Poems from this book have been published in *The Beloit Poetry Journal, Blackbird Online, Black Rock & Sage, Blue Sofa, The Cape Rock, The Comstock Review, Connecticut Review, Coracle, Gaia, The Long Islander, The MacGuffin, Marin Poetry Center Anthology, MARGIE, Pedestal, Ploughshares, PoetryBay, Poetry East, Rattapallax, RUNES, A Review of Poetry, sidereality, Sow's Ear Poetry Review, The Spoon River Poetry Review, Southern California Anthology, Texas Poetry Calendar 2002*, and *Tundra*.

For my children — Dan, Michael, Amy, Maggie,
Maureen, and Dave — and for their children —
Ben, Eli, Sophie, Theo, Jake, Spencer, Noah, Sam, Charlie,
Becca, Paul, and Abby

"Contrariwise," continued *Tweedledee, "if it was so, it might be; and if it were so, it would be; but as it isn't, it ain't. That's logic."*

— Lewis Carroll

CONTENTS

CONTRARIWISE

(*)   This symbol is used to indicate that a stanza has been divided because of pagination.

Ruskin's Advice to Charles Dodgson

What we like *determines what we* are . . .
— John Ruskin

Flowers all. Crocus its head barely raised above ground.
Tulip nodding, soft skirt petaled on the hillside.
Lilac, a ruffled scent. You breathe it in
Before you see it.
Pansy and sweet alyssum, riot and pallor
Entwined in the shade.
Daffodil — early and bright yet quick to fade.

Never the rose or peony whose lushness fills summer
Nor waxen water lily, still life open to sun
And closed into darkness.

Trust the delicate bouquet of the woodland:
Buttercup, bluebell, meadow foam.
Don't ask them to grace your parlor or tea
Where they will droop and wither.
Blossoms should be left
Innocent in their beds, as nature intended,
For us to admire. Ever part of the wild undefended.

Tulips

In dreams, the child says, what I eat
or drink tastes better than in life.
Fresher, cleaner. Apple skins are purple,
peaches red.

If I'm face-down, the child continues,
dream-food is black and white.
Fruit trees attach
to clouds, to circles inside circles
without color. And there's
a girl with white hair who
wears a black dress with white tulips.
Then I roll, blink everything
into color, so I can walk
where orchard trunks are violet
and bright green and yellow.
As I wave good-bye to
the girl in the tulip dress,
the sun shines blue. Around me,

apples purple and peaches turn red.
So I pick them, peel them
with my teeth, and bite down until
the sweetness colors me.

The Real Alice

It shall not touch with breath of bale
The pleasance of our fairy-tale.
— Lewis Carroll

              All our secrets — even the birthday
and unbirthday gifts exposed in black-and-white.
In that book, he made me blond. Made me tall, then tiny —
made me feel slower than I was, made me feel
like *she* felt in the Wood Where Things Have No Names:
wondering who I was or how I got there and why I
had a bosom now and body hair and how old
I had to be before I could marry him.
When I was small, we never talked of those things.
Except to joke that sister Edith wanted
to marry Papa. (And when we told her that was
impossible, she said she'd marry Mama.) Mr. Dodgson
and I did play, though, where I'd be Mama and tell
him not to be late and to wash the black stains
off his hands. Still, I called him Mister or Sir —
and only sometimes one of my pet names. You forget he had
sisters, knew about girls, and was twenty-six
when we first met. While Alice seemed to be me, he
was the White Knight, inventing, tripping, stammering.
So I took care of him. Wouldn't let Ina and Edith
tease. But the best wasn't the stories or when he
made me laugh as I sat on his knee.
The best was standing on a wood box in the glow
of his darkroom. He said he loved the soap smell
in my hair, that I smelled girlish. But *I* loved how
the wicked smell of silver nitrate and colloidion
made me feel a little drunk
as we stood side by side watching the developing pan
shiver up its images of me. The eyes came in first.
Then the hair. Think about the Cheshire Cat appearing.
And we'd stand there, he and I, breathing synchronized.
He was always looking for the unplanned —
a curl, bare toes from beneath a gown, tip of a tongue.
And it was just us. There, holding chemical-stained hands
*

away from my body, he'd arm-hug me, give me
Eskimo kisses, talk to me as people only can in the dark.
But he was never improper.
                              Sometimes, as I was growing older,
as we stood touching elbows, he'd say he'd wait for me.
That was our fairy tale. Before he took something I
never got back. Afterwards, I was no longer just the Liddell's
middle daughter. Worst of all, I no longer knew where she —
that Alice — stopped and I began. I wanted myself back.
And I wanted him not to belong to the world. Then Mama
destroyed all his letters. So when you see the last
photograph he took, the one where I'm eighteen and
glowering, please understand I was struggling to remember
how it was before everything changed,
before we slipped from a land of wonder to Wonderland.

Water Lily

Night is approaching. The air scented
and pollened yellow.
Edges are indistinct.
Surrounded by an ivory blossom
with fierce stamens, dappled, gnat-freckled,
she's furled by the lily.
There, a spiral of light, folded into the rods
and cones of its golden eye.
No longer restless, she draws up
her knees, idles where
beauty is pure and joy has form.

This is where she was before she began,
in darkness, knees to her chest,
a rounded, rose-nippled girl-seed
not yet desperate for light.
Dreaming of liquid warmth
and gentle hands, knowing only the imprint
of calyx and pistil, of unrealized petals.
Damp and smooth and unsuspecting.
Not yet impatient
for ripeness, not yet rooting
wildly toward an idea of flower.

Photographing the Alices

All mimsy were the borogoves,
And the mome raths outgrabe.
— Lewis Carroll

'Twas brillig. Oh, the sweetness of skin and lips.
        always speak the truth and write it down afterwards
What attracted me? Their trust. Innocence.
        croquet balls were live hedgehogs   mallets live flamingos
So many of them: the Alices — one Miss Muffet after another.
        what are the tarts made of   pepper and treacle
Modesty. Grace. An unmarked slate.
        you should learn not to make personal remarks
What each of us is before . . . the little girls, at least.
        how queer everything is today
For the photographs, you see, one had to hold still.
        oh my fur and whiskers
Not natural for boys. Always an ant or beetle to squash.
        it's exactly like a riddle with no answer
And less anxious to please. But the Alices — oh . . .
        it takes all the running you can do to keep in the same place
Much has been made of the Liddell girl, that dark sprite.
        let's pretend the glass has got all soft like gauze
Yet each in turn, in the eye of the lens, was a jewel of perfection.
        it was just like a conjuring trick
Xie, for instance, or Agnes — Dymphna or the Hatch girls.
        the prettiest are always further
Bewitching and bewitched. Not in need of a sword or shield to pose.
        a face is what one goes by generally
Skin like silk, so pale and poreless. Boys smelled like wet dog.
        throwing cold water over you would be better
Pose a girl, she stayed still, exposed. Quiet and self-contained.
        what does it matter where my body happens to be
Untouched. Still, each one a would-be — ripe apples looming.
        if you don't hold your tongues   I'll pick you
And, aware of the cold-blooded in me, I wanted . . . I loved . . .
        we're all mad here   I'm mad   you're mad
But chaste. Awed. No wish to spoil the unsullied.
        who in the world am I   ah   that's the great puzzle
        *

Yet they all betrayed me. Even Xie, vixen ahead of her years.
off with his head   off with her head
Despite much transitory perfection. A negative of a positive.
jam tomorrow and jam yesterday   but never jam today

Considering Pussywillow

> *Endurance is nobler than strength* . . .
> — John Ruskin

Take goose feathers to suck away lightning.
Cull spider webs and burn them.
Use blue to fend off witches,
bay leaves to bring back love.

Pussywillow crosshatched
and furred branches meshed as I
crept from bed to whistle past
the graveyard, infiltrate into night.

Restless as the tip of a cat's tail,
duller than a widow woman's ax,
cool as a dead man's hand,
older than a tree, older than God,

brushing off eye-diamonds, I cradled
the horns of the setting moon,
chanted for the child. Then I kept
watch, because a dream of fire cancels magic.

Wild Heart

I am the martyr. Just try the taking
instead of the sitting!
— Julia Margaret Cameron

Like Wordsworth I am always looking for
Emotion recollected in tranquility
Not the literal truth but the truth below
The truth
Quest or romance where
Any ordinary girl
Can be taken in the glass house

In each is my own filmy youth reborn
Idylls of sun-dusted flesh
Phases of the moon
Suggestive madonna
Daunting yet undaunted
All beauty arrested
Wild heart stilled one moment for us both

Asphodel

A ragged tutu,
green bled white at the folds,
fringe of a bodice pulling
out and down. Inversion.
And the black mouth with its
satin stain.
Yes, I said, now.
Here. The center will hold.
My eyes hypnotized
by apparent depth,
then released.
Now I will do anything.
Lift the stem — yes,
flex it, rock it back.
From black to green to white.
And there at the rim
exhalation of whimpering pink,
one more unconscious release.

A System of Rules for Conducting Tournaments Which Shall Fairly Award a Prize to the Most Winsome Child

> *Gain=Loss–Nil — a most desirable result.*
> — Charles Lutwidge Dodgson

Choose a winner? The loveliest girl child? *Much of a muchness.*
Having done it for Lawn Tennis, why not for females who come to tea?
A group of 28 is preferable, divided into sets of 4. See: I have 2 knees.
Ruskin will be happy to help me out by offering his 2 knees.
Let each girl despoil herself in her best frock and petticoat.
Each adorned with a suitable array of curls and wiles. *Twinkle, twinkle* . . .
Sit each on a knee for 30 seconds, allowing 15 seconds for changing knees.

Look them over. Steal a kiss from each. *Sentence first — verdict afterwards.*
Up and down. On and off with a satisfying amount of lap frottage.
There shall be no extra time for dropped gloves, hair bows, or tears.
We shall have a fair system for rating winsomeness.
In case of tie, the winners will have to sit on all 4 knees again.
Darlings all: what *fun* this tournament shall be. *Eat me, drink me.*
Girls are enchanting when they are still trusting and innocent.
Each one a possible winner. There will be no advance ranking.

Dare I consider this a game of chance/choice/cherry-picking?
Once the girls have begun to rotate and compete: bliss.
Decide then who shall win the prize, rated on charm and beauty.
Give extra points for wit and an air of sauciness. *Faster, faster.*
Such a delicious game. A marvel of minxes. A posy of pixies.
Oh, yes to hold each on each knee until, in 8.75 minutes —
Net — game, set match. Score: Love/Love. And who wins? Why I do.

Wild Oats

Katydid, cricket, beetle,
grasshopper in wild oats —
melody of midsummer's night.

And in the air
a calligraphy of midges,
male and female,
a green-black, stylized cloud

scrolled over stagnant water
whining and whining
a high-pitched, monotone refrain.

Xie: My Dear Multiplication Sign

My Whole's a victim I design
To photograph when days are fine.
— Charles Dodgson

Alice. I am so weary of hearing about Alice.
For all I care, she could have
stayed down the rabbit hole. I, too,
posed in the gypsy dress with one bud showing,
but on a chaise longue. And bare-limbed.
And don't called me "Z." Say "Ex-ey"; and it was,
of course, the X that made him call me
what he did. So you want to know if Mr. D.
touched me and if so where? Or if he kissed
me the same way he kissed Atty Owen.
Or if I posed naked like those bohemian
Hatch girls. I thought, for once, you'd want to ask
about our pug dog Snub, about my famous father
the Dean (Alice isn't the only girl
whose father was a dean). Or about *Mother*.
Now there's a subject. She bought girl-things
to add to his costume collection, things Mr. D.
felt were unseemly for a single man to
purchase. And Mother gave him my old clothes.
Sewed collars on them. (He liked us in
outsize collars.) For him, Mother bought
children's stockings in four sizes (dark, so they
wouldn't make our legs look gouty),
and found the acrobat costumes I refused
to wear. But I posed as a Chinese coolie,
a fur-trimmed Ophelia, a boy,
a poet named Penelope, two Millais oils
(*Asleep* turned out better than *Awake*),
and stood again and again with my violin.
The last time, at sixteen, in velvet. And I was
good at gazing into the camera.
A natural. The camera, not Mr. D., was
the lover I was too young to have. Only hold still
for sixty seconds and stare, the way you
will into the eyes of the rich and handsome man
you wish to marry. Not allowed
*

to move or blink as Mr. D. rushed about,
his photographic plates dripping and foul.
No sniffing, though, and no smiles — a smile
might make my face quiver. Violin bow
against the wall, so it wouldn't shake.
Then practice French verbs in my head
or recite Coleridge to myself. And I still haven't
told you anything? Well, Mother wrote
letters to him, played his word games.
Maybe she was half in love. But you want to know
about me. Did he touch me?
Yes, to arrange my hair, the folds of a costume.
And did his fingers linger?
Well, just look at the pictures. (Beautiful,
don't you think? And alluring. Those eyes!
Especially the parasol picture
when I was sixteen.) Yes, though he was
old, I liked him, especially when Mother was
jealous. And she was. But no, I seldom
sat in his lap. No . . . I won't explain.
And as for the rest — I don't have to tell
you more. But you're asking me about
Alice again. If you want to know *that*, ask Alice.
She'll talk to anyone, tell everything
she knows. Though she's much older
than I, she doesn't know much.
And, besides, Mr. D. always told everyone
that to get a truly superior photograph,
"Take a lens and put Xie before it."

Tomatoes

Seeds of change sprout in dark of the moon,
magic in my head. Surreal,
they burgeon, swelling to
tomatoes (Earliana, Brandywine,
Brimmer, Oxheart) lolling on vines
drawn toward light. And I
dance amid them
singing like the immortal child
I was, a pagan — god unto herself —
who sported shamelessly
(pressing a palm
to her own heart, ruddy
and many-chambered like a tomato),
started early, seeking potions
and seeds that might grow her into
one who could round, then ripen.

The New Model

> *There's only one kind of painting. It is the painting*
> *that presents the eye with perfection . . .*
> — William Bouguereau

scarlet (mercuric iodine) cassius red (tin bioxide and gold protoxide)

Apple, I think, as I sit sidesaddle on another girl's back,
Trying to be as good as Papa said I was,
Yet I've been here so long, and lunch was only for him.

sap green (unripe buckthorn) smalt (powdered cobalt glass)

Pear, I think. If I am good, he may give me one for myself.
When he tells me the story of Cupid with his arrows
And Psyche, I listen but beneath me I feel moving bones.

ochre (hydrated ferric oxide) verdigris (copper acetate)

I am trying not to fall. Peach, I think, or a few centimes.
You look, he tells me, *like a Raphael angel*.
But I don't know any M. Raphael or any angels.

purple red (mercuric chromate) brown madder (charred iron)

Now I am falling. Plums, I think, or a pair of new shoes.
Though I am being good, I want to scratch my nose,
And something is itching up between my legs.

viridian (sulfate of lime) scheele's green (copper arsenate)

What I'd like, maybe, is a pomegranate or a dog.
My bare foot is scribbled with ants. Down my cheek
A tear runs and salts my lips. Some marzipan,

indian yellow (caged cow urine) orpiment (arsenic sulfide)

Perhaps, shaped like a buttercup. This ride is too long,
And I want to get off. I need to make pipi.
Biscuits, I think, and buttermilk. But only if I'm good.

brown madder (iron) silver white (lead carbonate)

I hate good. Now I am smelling his body and the body
Of the other girl — Chérie, she's called — my body, too.
Again, he tells me, I have the face of an angel.

sienna (ochreous earth and manganese) orange (charred ceruse)

Angel food, I think, with berries. One day, he says,
When I grow bigger and rounder, he will paint me again.
Make me his Psyche. Cherries, I think, and arrows,

vermillion (mercuric sulfide) cassel earth (coal)

Like ones Cupid shoots. *One day I will paint you without
Clothes*, he tells me, and I think I might have to die first.
Or maybe, old smelly man that he is, he will.

ivory black (charred ivory) mummy (asphaltum and bone ash)

Pomegranate

Falling birds as white scraps of paper,
The mountain spiking a wreath of fog.

A promise, like a pomegranate,
Bleeds when it is cut,

This blood-letting more painful than most.
Each seed another bitter sweet. Don't

Count them. Counting only confuses the future.
Consider terror, yet don't give in.

Let the paper birds fly. Let the bloody seeds
Burst. Let the fog keep all its secrets.

It's All Greek

> *Lo! with a little rod,*
> *I did but touch the honey of romance —*
> *And must I lose a soul's inheritance?*
> — Oscar Wilde

Yes, until proved otherwise: innocent, innocent . . .
Not a lover, more a connoisseur of slender works of art.

The form of a cat or cat o' nine tails. Or of a long-necked
porcelain vase, sleek, newly-laid with Greek keys.

Ah, the Greeks had it right, after all, oiling the naked
boy bodies, crowning them lightly with laurel or olive.

There are sins of commission and omission. Of the two, I
prefer the latter. Boy-becoming/man-not-yet-finished.

Before you judge me, I admit to nothing and everything:
revision/reversion/perversion/inversion/illusion.

Illusion is the first of all pleasures. Not only knee breeches
or velvet but flesh close to the bone. And I — a slut for Beauty.

Lilac

The day is a transparent umbrella
I angle above our heads
as the sky rains frogs and spiders.

Unphased, we stroll past moat and lilac,
rulers of a mythical kingdom.

While the unconscious shrink from
this nightmare
of ancient Biblical plagues,

our day is a transparent umbrella
upended to catch the chaos
that would agitate the moat.

Frogs trill a song of heady freedom
as spiders veil the lilac.

Cloaked in silk, hymned, we walk
a riot of beauty, protected by
the transparent umbrella of day.

J.M. Looks for Alice in Neverland

> **Hook**: *Pan, who and what are thou?*
> **Peter**: *I'm youth. I'm joy. I'm a little bird*
> *that has broken out of the egg.*
> — J.M. Barrie

Girl little girl where are you
Mother little mother speak

Fearsome the pirates
Fickle the fairies
Slippery my shadow

How doth the little crocodile
How dense is the dark of the moon
How many miles to Babylon

Not Darling but Pleasance
Kitten or flamingo in her arms

Wild the weather
Fragile my heart
Chaste the looking glass

Who wants a button or kiss
Who wants to fly
Who will read me and take me to bed

Sweet girl who can't grow up
Alice little mother I'm here

Azalea Wild

Rhododendron, rose, and azalea wild,
An innocent midsummer evening's bower —
Dense of leaf and thick with flower,
A bed for a light-dazzled naked child.
Around him: camellia and buttercup,
Pale moss too fragile for human feet,
A full moon to glower, new lambs to bleat,
And the hawthorn bush where the fairies sup.

Not truly benign. Don't wait for the dawn.
Consider the bee, the thorn, the nettle,
The trackless wood, the fairies' mettle.
Snatch the babe from this nest before he's gone.

Beatrix Potter: On Children and Love

Now run along, and don't get into mischief.
— Mrs. Rabbit

My rabbits and mice, squirrels, cats, and ducks:
Bad mannered, sometimes ill-tempered.
Nervous or fierce creatures all.

A twitch of bunnies
A peck of hens
A snarl of foxes
A screech of mice
A scrabble of moles
A squeal of pigs
A pounce of kittens
A chatter of squirrels
A prickle of hedgehogs

And still, despite all, less bother than any child.
With my creatures, no spit or snot, screams or dreams,
No inconvenient incontinence or waste.

For he who would dare to love a human child:

A tangle of time and disarray,
A maze with shadowed paths of pain.

Dream Book

Its leaves are bay laurel,
Words the pollen of the rose.
      Count me in
Don't put the key in the wrong latch.
Don't forget to tie a string.
      Tell me the dream book
Once my mother marred it with her sighs,
My brother stole it,
My father drank his whiskey.
      Will tomorrrow come
If tales leak into margins,
If ink is both sea and sky?
      If nothing opens
Will pollen lose its breath,
And will the leaves all turn to ash?

Summer 1893: Little Lord Fauntleroy Meets Alice Liddell

*I was a perfectly normal boy. I got myself
just as damn dirty as the other boys.*
— Vivian Burnett

Where are your curls? she asked. *And those velvet knee breeches?*

She, Alice, stout and with an dog-head umbrella. No magic here.
No poetry of thought. Thin lips, powdered smell of old woman.

You'll never live this down. Trust me. It'll follow you always.

The White Rabbit and Caterpillar lost. Tweedledee lost. too.
And no curious girl in pinafore eager to illuminate Wonderland.

Like that suit with the big collar. And you have a sissy name, too.

Together, I thought we'd enjoy an idyllic Mad Hatter's tea,
move around chair by chair, cup by cup, talking about our stolen lives.

An English Lord? she said. *Your voice twangs and your accent's horrid.*

Oh God, I'm drinking gin with a woman who criticizes everything
and barks like my old governess. Yes . . . Alice has *become* the Red Queen.

Why so quiet? Cat got your tongue? 'Twas your Dearest did this to you.

Too much growl and bite. So, suddenly, I begin to chase the Cheshire
Cat, desperate to fade from Alice's book and then from my own.

Goldenrod

Morning. Dragon clouds stalk the sky.
Snake uncoils on lichen
flicking his tongue to sense the day.
As wind shuffles goldenrod,
I discard old myths,
steep brown, edge into shadow,
poise unmoving — knees faintly bowed —
until I am the doe, alert to heat
and shriek of day, who waits for

Night. The marsh, an inland sea,
shines in moonlight; wet bark
curls witch-fingers from
outstretched arms.
Eager to prowl, I shed new myths,
bleach yellow. As I chuff,
my tufted feet crimp
silvered grass circling
the doe who can no longer flee.

Alice in Storyville

I always spent every cent I got.
— E. J. Bellocq

Yes, I see my life through a lens. Insane, people call me,
or dwarfish. The Toulouse-Lautrec of N' Orleans.
Lies. I am and always was of normal size.
Storyville is my quarter, the working girls —
sweet Alices — I tip my hat to them
before I press their bodies onto my dark plates.
Unspoiled in their cribs, they like my manners,
diamond stickpins and red cravats.
And I, *mon dieu*, love their honeyed skin, sweet berries,
round limbs, and birds' nests down below.
What I want: to see through the looking glass.
What they want: a frieze of time,
colorless and without sound or smell or taste or pain.
Each in her photograph: a Mardi Gras queen, bare Rapunzel,
a child Magdalene with an aura but no orifices,
arrested before the ravage of time or disease.
I let them wear Mama's locket yet never touch them.
Spend my money on drink and fusions and ornaments,
so my degradation and theirs are tangential.
Only in my chambers — in a *ménage à moi* — do I
enjoy *les demoiselles*. Clutched in my right hand, a flat image
of a girl, pure and revirgined, while below
my sinister hand slowly fulfills its own unholy inclinations.

Imago

Think not of fire then and catastrophe
but of the elegant luna moth.

In larval life, as caterpillar, it ate
and ate, self-centered

and greedy. Now after sleep, it unfolds
from its cocoon, a delicate imago

the color of a new leaf. From a distance
a moonlit opium-sprite,

yet up close, fierce of face, a nightmare,
hungry phantom with no mouth, silent

and round-eyed, helpless to change its fate,
flying like us toward light,

toward flirtation and death.
The flame, quickfire and chaos —

a lurid struggle to avoid . . . because
beauty snared, loses luster, loses all.

Billy Moon

I'm not going to do Nothing any more.
— Christopher Robin

The English, alas, treat their offspring like:
Donkeys (be still) or piglets (eat) or bears (don't bite).

I was, though called Moon, the Milnes' Rosemary-
Girl and then, Father's Christopher — lip with curl.

Small and slight and dressed in smocks,
To defend myself, I learned to box

And talk, like Alice, of the ache of fame,
Soul used and used up with the theft of my name.

The English, alas, treat their offspring like:
Donkeys (don't twitch), piglets (bathe) or bears (not right).

Meadow Foam

Here in the moon palace,
wrapped in snow soft as meadow foam,
unwrinkled, unconcerned, unrepentant,
toes warm, wide eyes frosted by haloes
of winter cloud, belly still,

I shall perhaps never risk
an uncoiled rope,
never blink, never permit
unmarked feet to feel the ground.

The Outsider Asks to Be Let In

> *I'll always be this way, always was.*
> — Henry Darger

To Irving Edwards of the Simplex Music Company:

I clean latrines for the sisters at St. Joseph's and investigate
Realms of the Unreal as well as cumulonimbus clouds.

But I think I can write song-poems for you, lovely pieces
about raw little girls from a world that is dark

and dangerous and perpetually at war. I do like girls —
celestial children — and would, if I could, adopt one.

Each girl a fresh martyr from God who fails to
protect her. Oh, I'd give my child wings and weapons

and 1000 balls of string to tie together so, in the worst
tornado, she could still find her way back home.

In my verse, I'd sing of what I can't have, *of ships and shoes
and sealing wax* and of the sister they took from a cabbage

and gave away when Mother died. At the asylum, before I
ran off, my name was *Crazy*, and they may have been right,

but believe me, Mr. Edwards, though I know storm and disaster,
I do have a wild and free pure-of-sin girl-loving song to sing.

Yours in fair weather, Henry Darger

Wisteria

Snow on wisteria vines: white fingers
from gnarled fists
as snap of live oak leaves
marks footfall of wild cat.
Outlines of your bare soles

head north toward the arbor,
a ghost house,
its ghost cat prowling
a floor of river stones
and breaching invisible walls.

23rd Psalm of the Vivians

We shall slam them with our wings.
— Henry Darger

Eeny meeny miney mo   my shepherd
Loves me loves not me
Boy girl boy girl
He is she is he wants she wants
There are green pastures here but I shall not want
Restoration
Take off my dress and put on the wings
This place may look like a pasture
But it's a battlefield
She was a little girl who had a little curl
Right up under her flowered dress
She was me unperturbed unrestored
So the girl says and   Have it your way
She never looks down or back
A paper doll of a girl boy girl
A paper tiger of a boy girl boy
Curiouser and curiouser
The shadow of confusion   she says   is yours not mine
I shall fear no evil
I may tie a sash   clip on barrettes
But I keep my sword under my dress
My rod and my staff they comfort me
Because I know where the bodies
Are buried and the curled-up secrets too
So I fear no evil
Goodness eeny meeny miney winged mercy mo
Boy girl boy girl girl
Love me or love me not   Have it your way
This is not a sad psalm

Redbud

Spokes of redbud branches overhead,
and two girls curve in a hollow.
As they sip sugar from blossoms,
splinters of sunlight prick their skin

An odd simultaneity, but I hover above,
both the watcher and the watched
where bud-lipped girls are part of a blink,
face-to-face, intermingling curls —
light and dark — into herringbone braids.
Then they weave their sashes together,
and, exhaling wildness,
the two, now one, gaze into mirrors

of facing pupils, see shapes ghosting
away. As they dip their heads forward,
they rub noses and gently,
touch each other tongue to tongue.

Painter of Insecure Infantas

The best way not to fall back into childhood is never to have left it.
— Balthus

Legs liquid with light, knickers exposed, and beneath, the hairless sex.
Yet they gossip about me, Count Balthasar Klossowski de Rola,
when I am not the subject. Balthus is. He, paintbrush poised to catch

androgyny, that edge between innocence and perversity.
They ask about this, taunt and invade B's scant privacy, gape
at his girl-wife or the infantas — Thérèse and the others. But, look,

B can walk through walls, ghostly flesh, incubus, his boy-self
inhabiting the portrait girl's body, its awkward, wide-faced dream.
If she opens her eyes, his soul may fly out. If she exposes her hands,

they may trespass. Magic is loss or the *crac*; and B, a leap-year child,
born as Rilke said in the *crac* of February, can be forever
quartered in a world where both age and love are phantoms.

And where clothing is costume, except the slip framing the slit,
communion veil of intimacy — its lacy edge proof of reality. Mix
the metaphor and veil becomes white flag of surrender. Others call

this warped, fail to see *him* there in *her*. Her ecstasy, the revenant's
leap toward pleasure in flesh. Ask the girl warm in her chair with
puss in her lap. She could explain. Or ask the cat. *M. Chat*,

B himself, grinning as he laps at cream. He is also a child
under a spell, the anesthetized, the enchanted glazed by color.
Laced fingers atop the head tend an invisible brush. She/He.

As is the cat. As is the chair. The girl who lies in the lap of the chair
shifts her position. Lucky chair. All girls are both found and lost.
All B portraits are of the self and layered in oil, in time,

in temperament. Not nymph or phantom. More Doppelgänger.
Or equation. Foreground is to background, left is to right
as girl is to chair as paint is to veil upon veil. Peel it away.

X-ray it. See the black cartoon beneath the unfinished cusp-child.
Use sleight of hand. Now you see, now you don't. Girl? Chair? Cat?
Knickers? Cream? *Crac?* Balthus, insecure, unfinished child . . . me.

Apples Drop, Smooth, Cheeky

Mornings, the air zig-zag with
Striped wings, I kneel on the littered

Ground, seeking my gift
From the tree, just one unbruised.

Apple — yes, ever since Eve, a way past
The tree, past fruited plain,

To snake eyes, then to the snake,
Chance to bite and be bitten.

Nights in the orchard, hoofs stir
Cider fumes as buck and doe

Mouth windfall. Then daylight again,
Heat, snake, a thrum of bees:

Coil of redness, of readiness, of a taste
For sting.

Dorothea Takes on Julia Margaret Cameron

Hands off! I do not molest what I photograph,
I do not meddle and I do not arrange.
— Dorothea Lange

      For Julia Margaret and her ilk,
Tennyson was a Sinatra, pop-singer poet,
and flights, like his, into excess applauded.
But why should girls or boys be used?
Oh, I'm not talking prurience,
just explicit and gorgeous fakery.
No child a possession. Rather the child as
a person, person becoming, person
who is, above all, natural.

      Does this offend? Should I
revere J.M., she — woman who wore
the diamond choke-chain of privilege,
who saw children as frozen jewels
upon that chain? No truth. A lens should be
classless, work spontaneous. Life in all its grit
and splendor. And love of beauty dispassionate
rather than willfully overdone.

Rosemary

What exists is here. Honeybee in rosemary,
pelican slamming a wave. The moment —

photograph frozen before it changes,
like the scallop from twelve million years ago

washed up this morning, a fossil on your beach.
You merge in and out of days traveling

parallel places in earthy yet subconscious worlds.
Passage of time is an illusion: young, old, sweet,

bitter, now, then, maybe, what if. Your reflection has
as much reality as you do. Embrace the lie.

His Baby Ballerinas

> *Ballet is woman.*
> — George Balanchine

because we are short of waist and long of leg
because we are elegant and thin
because we look like fresh-faced boys in tutus
because we sip water but swallow little food

we are so light we no longer bleed
we dance and dance and even in sleep we dance
dance through sadness and pain
dance to be the girl — yes, girl — Mr. B. loves most

our bodies bow to his commands and our demands
minds think only of elevation and *port de bras*
souls, free-floating, are slick now with sweat and rosin
our unconditional hearts are palmed by Mr. B.

our sisters eat chocolates and chips and have breasts
they run through fields with wind in their hair
they read books and have hours to waste
in the backseats of cars they drink Bud and kiss boys

but we bend and worship at the altar of Mr. B.
tired and tense and wary we have only volition
we are hungry and stunted except behind footlights
no longer his babies — now we are old children

Poppies

Thresh your way
Through the nodding poppies.
Search for the honey bear,
The stealthy fox blue-washed
By the setting moon,
Like all else,
You'll lose them in shadow
Before morning. Loss is
A ghost path through deep grass,
Its forks, its finite lines,
Its disappearance.
And you can dream it,
Angle through cloud,
Wake from the dream
And, awake now, dream it again.

Taking the Fifth

> *I'm in the milk and the milk's in me.*
> — Maurice Sendak

Because of a boy named Mickey, I've been accused of almost everything.
Full-frontal nudity in the Night Kitchen. Quite perverse, they said.
Think of the possibilities — milk bottles, liver, butter, dough —
a boy and his penis might want to explore at night.

A childless (and single) man who is obsessed with the lives
of children is bad enough without what springs up when one considers
a boy's naked body. In my case, the whispers became murmurs
became roars until there was a rolling of eyes and a gnashing of teeth

as I moved in an instant from suspect to possibly guilty as charged.
I have the right to remain silent. Anything I say can and will be held
against me. But my mother and father — wherever they are —
can vouch for me, as well as all who have ever heard the call

of the wild things. Listen, I swear, the only child I've ever loved
or abused is my own feral and still unheroically unrefined self.

Leaves

In the pond shallows, my feet — no longer
full-fleshed and firm — are
pale-veined leaves, slowly yellowing.

Water, too, is yellow in midmorning light
and wedges of hard-eyed
minnows surge forward to nip my toes.

Later it will be hot. Later it will be
later. But not yet, I hope,
too late. A squint turns the sun-starred pond

to snow; and I can feel winter, its freeze
and thaw. How lost leaves become
decoupage in ice. How the past is unforgiven;

and how — even in cold — the memory of light
and new leaf and fresh skin still burn.

Selektion: The Painted Girl

> *I'm interested in the stage of a human being where it's not so*
> *important whether it's a male or female, before we can tell any*
> *social background or anything, it's just . . . abstract, almost.*
> — Gottfried Helnwein

like a negative bled dark   left too long   in searing light

it's blue   all blue   and the blurred child   walks amid

a street of bodies   her scant dress white   lips pursed

listening perhaps   to the blue flute   of a distant piper

the dead in coats and scarves   it's cold   but her feet

bare   arms held from her sides   and everything's blue

her head   injured head   gauze-wrapped   no face

blinded here   but is it worse   than the other place

where she knelt   wearing white panties   dark eyes

masked   by her own cupped hands   black-and-white

here   the only blues inside   where to go   what to do

but whose child is this   who will confess   piper

whose child   turned monochrome   how will she

bear up   pay   why must we select   our children

Crown of Clover

This wood — oak, beech, and spindle —
So sharp in winter, so blurred when trees releaf.

In the pond, a singing frog and silent lily.
What then was the moment of the turn?

In the near meadow, onion, bluebell, clover —
And where have they been hidden?

At dusk, you light a candle, arc wood and glade
In its waver of gold. At dawn, you blow it out.

But who will peel the onion, weave a crown of clover,
Watch the water lily dip its deckled skirt?

Who will lie in grass beneath the spindle tree?
Who will make a fête of this yellow-green day?

A Grave Lecture from Vladimir

The cradle rocks above an abyss . . .
— Vladimir Nabokov

Was it Shaw who once said the rumors of his death had been greatly exaggerated? Or Mark Twain? Does it matter? It was Shaw, I know, who said he liked children as well as flowers but didn't cut off their heads and put them in pots.

So while rumors of *my* death are *true*, yes, I still hover about here smacking my disembodied lips not over the human condition but over the prepossessing beauty of little butterflies. I didn't start it, of course. Even the girl baby learning to walk plays the vamp.

Don't blame me. I'm only the messenger. And what is the message? There's nothing like the butterfly — achingly female — with its promise of future sex. Remember how old M. Chevalier sang, "Thank heaven for little girls."

Thank *hell*, I say, if you've ever had to deal with them. Manipulative devils paving the way to the underworld=underwearworld with mischief or bad intentions. Why, actually, I never much liked real children.

What I most loved and hated and adored and suffered and desired (yet never pursued) was the glowing heat of woman pulsing through the seemingly innocent body of a luscious, juicy young girl. Boys run cold but girls run hot. And hotter.

Lolita? Who is she? Alice? Yes. Wendy? No. Eve — of course. Saint and whore, kitten and cat. Complain about me as an incorrigible, dirty old man. Single out the voyeurs as well as the perps (some gent=gender differences here).

But your bitching is abominably misplaced. We are lambs — all of us — (tho sometimes wolves in lambskin) led to the slaughter by Bo Peeps or Bo Peters (I'm bored now with the butterfly metaphor), tenders of Everyman's wet dream.

Honeysuckle Dream

A hut of clay and wattles
A bee-loud glade
We shall write
Upon the still water
And see words slowly vapor
Toward the sky
And then we'll lie together
Rapt with wings
As always out of time

. . . let's consider who it was that dreamed . . .

Begin at the beginning . . . and go on until you come to the end: then stop.

— Lewis Carroll

BIOGRAPHY

Susan Terris's poetry books include *Natural Defenses* (Marsh Hawk Press), *Fire Is Favorable to the Dreamer* (Arctos Press), *Poetic License* (Adastra Press), *Curved Space* (La Jolla Poets Press), and *Eye of the Holocaust* (Arctos Press). Her work has appeared in *Iowa Review*, *Field*, *Calyx*, *The Journal*, *Colorado Review*, *Prairie Schooner*, *Shenandoah*, *Denver Quarterly*, *Southern California Anthology*, and *Ploughshares*. With CB Follett, she is coeditor of an annual anthology, *RUNES, A Review of Poetry*. Her prize-winning chapbooks include *Block Party* (Pudding House Publications) and *Marriage License* (Pavement Saw Press). Among her many awards are the George Bogin Memorial Prize, from the Poetry Society of America, plus prizes from the *Florida Review*, *Many Mountains Moving*, *Literal Latte*, *Salt Hill*, *Southern California Anthology*, *Spoon River*, and the Faulkner/Wisdom Poetry Competition. She is also the winner of a Pushcart Award for her poem "Goldfish: A Diptych," published in *Field*.

OTHER POETRY AND SHORT FICTIONS
AVAILABLE FROM TIME BEING BOOKS

YAKOV AZRIEL
Threads from a Coat of Many Colors: Poems on Genesis

EDWARD BOCCIA
No Matter How Good the Light Is: Poems by a Painter

LOUIS DANIEL BRODSKY
The Capital Café: Poems of Redneck, U.S.A.
Catchin' the Drift o' the Draft *(short fictions)*
Combing Florida's Shores: Poems of Two Lifetimes
The Complete Poems of Louis Daniel Brodsky: Volumes One–Three
Disappearing in Mississippi Latitudes: Volume Two of *A Mississippi Trilogy*
The Eleventh Lost Tribe: Poems of the Holocaust
Falling from Heaven: Holocaust Poems of a Jew and a Gentile *(Brodsky and Heyen)*
Forever, for Now: Poems for a Later Love
Four and Twenty Blackbirds Soaring
Gestapo Crows: Holocaust Poems
A Gleam in the Eye: Poems for a First Baby
Leaky Tubs *(short fictions)*
Mississippi Vistas: Volume One of *A Mississippi Trilogy*
Mistress Mississippi: Volume Three of *A Mississippi Trilogy*
Nuts to You! *(short fictions)*
Once upon a Small-Town Time: Poems of America's Heartland
Paper-Whites for Lady Jane: Poems of a Midlife Love Affair
Peddler on the Road: Days in the Life of Willy Sypher
Pigskinizations *(short fictions)*
Rated Xmas *(short fictions)*
Shadow War: A Poetic Chronicle of September 11 and Beyond, Volumes
    One–Five
Showdown with a Cactus: Poems Chronicling the Prickly Struggle
    Between the Forces of Dubya-ness and Enlightenment, 2003–2006
This Here's a Merica *(short fictions)*
The Thorough Earth
Three Early Books of Poems by Louis Daniel Brodsky, 1967–1969: *The Easy
    Philosopher, "A Hard Coming of It" and Other Poems*, and *The Foul Rag-
    and-Bone Shop*
Toward the Torah, Soaring: Poems of the Renascence of Faith
A Transcendental Almanac: Poems of Nature
Yellow Bricks *(short fictions)*
You Can't Go Back, Exactly
Voice Within the Void: Poems of *Homo supinus*

866-840-4334

HTTP://WWW.TIMEBEING.COM

HARRY JAMES CARGAS *(editor)*
Telling the Tale: A Tribute to Elie Wiesel on the Occasion of His 65th
 Birthday — Essays, Reflections, and Poems

JUDITH CHALMER
Out of History's Junk Jar: Poems of a Mixed Inheritance

GERALD EARLY
How the War in the Streets Is Won: Poems on the Quest of Love and Faith

GARY FINCKE
Blood Ties: Working-Class Poems

CHARLES ADÉS FISHMAN
Blood to Remember: American Poets on the Holocaust *(editor)*
Chopin's Piano

CB FOLLETT
Hold and Release

ALBERT GOLDBARTH
A Lineage of Ragpickers, Songpluckers, Elegiasts & Jewelers: Selected
 Poems of Jewish Family Life, 1973–1995

ROBERT HAMBLIN
From the Ground Up: Poems of One Southerner's Passage to Adulthood
Keeping Score: Sports Poems for Every Season

WILLIAM HEYEN
Erika: Poems of the Holocaust
Falling from Heaven: Holocaust Poems of a Jew and a Gentile *(Brodsky and Heyen)*
The Host: Selected Poems, 1965–1990
Pterodactyl Rose: Poems of Ecology
Ribbons: The Gulf War — A Poem

TED HIRSCHFIELD
German Requiem: Poems of the War and the Atonement of a Third Reich Child

866-840-4334

HTTP://WWW.TIMEBEING.COM

VIRGINIA V. JAMES HLAVSA
Waking October Leaves: Reanimations by a Small-Town Girl

RODGER KAMENETZ
The Missing Jew: New and Selected Poems
Stuck: Poems Midlife

NORBERT KRAPF
Blue-Eyed Grass: Poems of Germany
Looking for God's Country
Somewhere in Southern Indiana: Poems of Midwestern Origins

ADRIAN C. LOUIS
Blood Thirsty Savages

LEO LUKE MARCELLO
Nothing Grows in One Place Forever: Poems of a Sicilian American

GARDNER MCFALL
The Pilot's Daughter

JOSEPH MEREDITH
Hunter's Moon: Poems from Boyhood to Manhood

BEN MILDER
The Good Book Also Says . . . : Numerous Humorous Poems Inspired by
    the New Testament
The Good Book Says . . . : Light Verse to Illuminate the Old Testament
Love Is Funny, Love Is Sad
The Zoo You Never Gnu: A Mad Menagerie of Bizarre Beasts and Birds

CHARLES MUÑOZ
Fragments of a Myth: Modern Poems on Ancient Themes

MICHEAL O'SIADHAIL
The Gossamer Wall: Poems in Witness to the Holocaust

866-840-4334

HTTP://WWW.TIMEBEING.COM

JOSEPH STANTON
A Field Guide to the Wildlife of Suburban Oʻahu
Imaginary Museum: Poems on Art